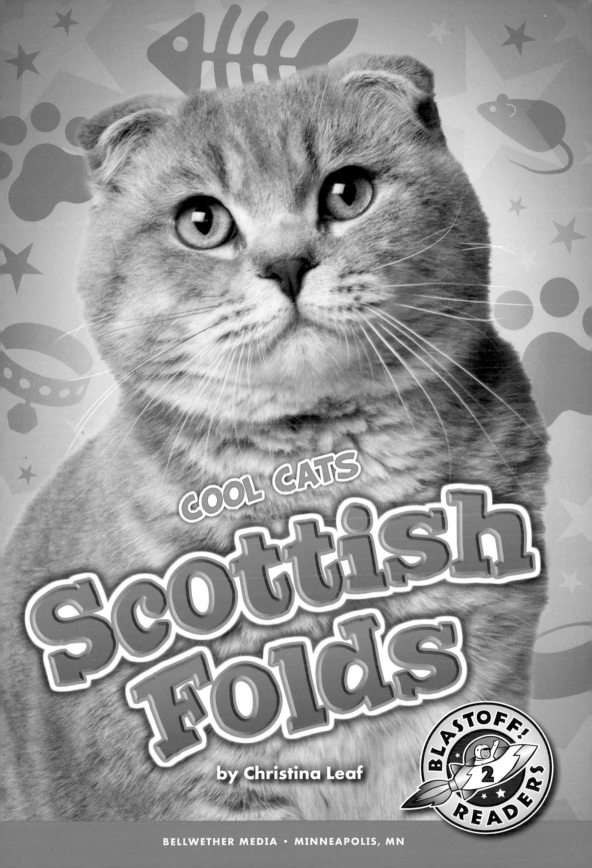

COOL CATS

Scottish Folds

by Christina Leaf

BELLWETHER MEDIA • MINNEAPOLIS, MN

Note to Librarians, Teachers, and Parents:

Blastoff! Readers are carefully developed by literacy experts and combine standards-based content with developmentally appropriate text.

Level 1 provides the most support through repetition of high-frequency words, light text, predictable sentence patterns, and strong visual support.

Level 2 offers early readers a bit more challenge through varied simple sentences, increased text load, and less repetition of high-frequency words.

Level 3 advances early-fluent readers toward fluency through increased text and concept load, less reliance on visuals, longer sentences, and more literary language.

Level 4 builds reading stamina by providing more text per page, increased use of punctuation, greater variation in sentence patterns, and increasingly challenging vocabulary.

Level 5 encourages children to move from "learning to read" to "reading to learn" by providing even more text, varied writing styles, and less familiar topics.

Whichever book is right for your reader, Blastoff! Readers are the perfect books to build confidence and encourage a love of reading that will last a lifetime!

This edition first published in 2016 by Bellwether Media, Inc.

No part of this publication may be reproduced in whole or in part without written permission of the publisher. For information regarding permission, write to Bellwether Media, Inc., Attention: Permissions Department, 5357 Penn Avenue South, Minneapolis, MN 55419.

Library of Congress Cataloging-in-Publication Data

Leaf, Christina, author.
  Scottish Folds / by Christina Leaf.
     pages cm. – (Blastoff! Readers. Cool Cats)
  Summary: "Relevant images match informative text in this introduction to Scottish folds. Intended for students in kindergarten through third grade"– Provided by publisher.
  Audience: Ages 5-8.
  Audience: K to grade 3.
  Includes bibliographical references and index.
  ISBN 978-1-62617-314-9 (hardcover : alk. paper)
  1. Scottish fold cat–Juvenile literature. 2. Cat breeds–Juvenile literature. I. Title. II. Series: Blastoff! readers. 2, Cool cats.
  SF449.S35L43 2016
  636.8–dc23
                            2015031554

Printed in the United States of America, North Mankato, MN.

Table of **Contents**

What Are Scottish Folds?

Scottish fold cats are known for their folded ears.

Some have ears that bend forward. Others have ears that lay flat.

The **breed** can be short-haired or long-haired.

Scottish Fold Coats

solid

tabby

bi-color

calico

Scottish fold **coats** come in many colors and patterns. They are often **solid** or **tabby**.

The first Scottish fold was from Scotland's Tayside **region**. She was a white barn cat called Susie. A **mutation** made her ears fold.

Scotland

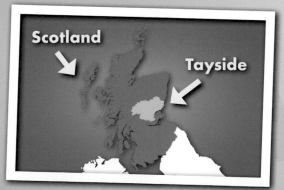

N
W E
S

Scotland

Tayside

A shepherd named William Ross noticed Susie in 1961.

Ross **bred** kittens from Susie. He called the breed "lop-eared" after a type of rabbit.

Later, the cats were renamed
Scottish folds. They are now
loved pets.

Folded Ears and Owl Looks

All Scottish folds are born with straight ears. Some ears fold around three weeks.

Only about half the
kittens get folded ears!

Those with straight ears help keep the breed healthy.

Scottish folds are charming pets
no matter what ears they have.

These medium-sized cats have round eyes and heads. People say they look like owls. The cats often look like they are smiling!

Scottish Fold Profile

— folded ears

— big, round eyes

— chubby cheeks

Weight: 6 to 13 pounds (3 to 6 kilograms)

Life Span: 13 to 16 years

Scottish folds do not say much.
Some talk with quiet chirps.

However, they are **affectionate**. These sweet cats cuddle with their favorite people.

Scottish folds have goofy **poses**. They stand on their back legs or flop on their backs.

Many **lounge** like humans.
They sit back with their paws
on their bellies!

Glossary

affectionate—loving

bred—purposely mated two cats to make kittens with certain qualities

breed—a type of cat

coats—the hair or fur covering some animals

lounge—to sit or rest in a lazy manner

mutation—a new form of something that has changed

poses—positions in which cats sit, stand, or lie down

region—a part of a country or the world

solid—one color

tabby—a pattern that has stripes, patches, or swirls of colors

To Learn More

AT THE LIBRARY

Dash, Meredith. *Scottish Fold Cats.* Minneapolis, Minn.: ABDO Kids, 2015.

Hengel, Katherine. *Sweet Scottish Folds.* Edina, Minn.: ABDO Pub. Co., 2012.

Miller, Connie Colwell. *Scottish Fold Cats.* Mankato, Minn.: Capstone Press, 2009.

ON THE WEB

Learning more about Scottish folds is as easy as 1, 2, 3.

1. Go to www.factsurfer.com.

2. Enter "Scottish folds" into the search box.

3. Click the "Surf" button and you will see a list of related web sites.

With factsurfer.com, finding more information is just a click away.

Index